This book is dedicated to my beloved husband, Harold DeLoach. He was able to keep the manuscript alive for two years while I was incapacitated with clinical depression. He did all the things necessary for the process of publishing my book. I am deeply grateful for the many sacrifices he made on my behalf; thus making this book a reality. He was my constant companion, care giver and encourager. For these things I want you to know how I appreciate you and love you for now and all eternity.

ACKNOWLEDGEMENTS

To Andy Stubblefield for the through job he did editing the manuscript.

To my sisters, Bennie Cornwell and Tammy Cooper and sister-in-laws Johnnie Mae Stice and Carol Sheets who came and kept our household going when I was unable.

To New Beginnings Sunday School Class, First Methodist Church who brought many meals and encouragement to Harold and I.

To Dr. Viadislav Yeganov and Dr. Joshua Warren for their patience and genuine interest for my medical care.

To sons, Dwain and Darren DeLoach for their love and unwavering support.

To my many friends on Facebook whose support and interest came in the way of cards, prayers, and photos.

To the Valley Mills Book Review Club that believed in me from the beginning to now.

The Valley Mills Library Book Review Group
The Thursday Morning Bible Study Group
The Light Brigade Writers Group

To Judy Janowski, a writer friend who has supported, believed, and encouraged me with the publication of Daily Bread of Life. Judy, the author of 'Life is a Garden Party is a trusted friend and mentor.

To Dr. Laura Wright who has been my faithful therapist for the past seven years. She is a wonderful Christian counselor and her insights into my life have affected me profoundly both then and now. I owe her a deep sense of gratitude.

Finally to God and His faithfulness, love and caring that was and is with me as we finalize plans for Daily Bread of Life.

THIS BOOK IS A MIRACLE. MIRACLES ARE FROM GOD FOR A PURPOSE. IT IS UP TO US TO DISCOVER WHAT THAT PURPOSE IS. I BELIEVE THAT THE PURPOSE OF THIS MIRACLE IS THAT MANY CAN BENEFIT FROM THE TALENT GOD HAS GIVEN SHERI IN THE SHARING OF BIBLICAL TRUTHS THROUGH THE DEVOTIONALS SHE HAS BEEN INSPIRED TO WRITE. IT HAS BEEN AN INCREDIBLE JOURNEY. THE REASONS FOR THE DELAY IN THE PUBLISHING OF THIS BOOK ARE MANY BUT THE PRIMARY REASON HAS BEEN HER HEALTH. SEVERAL YEARS AGO SHERI DEVELOPED A CONDITION KNOWN AS CLINICAL DEPRESSION A VERY DEBILITATING DISEASE THAT ROBS THE BODY AND THE SOUL OF MOST ALL OF THE SENSES AND WHAT MAKES US ABLE TO FUNCTION. THERE IS NO DEFINITIVE CAUSE AND NO DEFINITIVE SOLUTION. WHAT IS LEFT ARE MULTIPLE TRIALS AND GUESSES AS TO WHAT CAN BE DONE TO HELP. SHERI HAD A MIGHTY BATTLE AND WE BELIEVE THAT ONLY A MIRACLE FROM GOD ALLOWED HER TO RECOVER. AS SHE BEGAN TO RECOVER HER FAMILY AND FRIENDS ENCOURAGED HER TO FINISH THIS BOOK. THROUGH THE EFFORTS OF MANY WE HAVE BEEN BLESSED TO ACCOMPLISH THIS CALLING. WE HUMBLY GIVE A GOD WHO " IS BIG ENOUGH " THE GLORY AND THE PRAISE FOR THIS. IT IS OUR DESIRE THAT YOU WILL DEVELOP A STRONGER PERSONAL RELATIONSHIP WITH GOD THROUGH THE DEVOTIONALS THAT FOLLOW.

HAROLD W DELOACH

PROVERBS, GOD'S WISDOM

READ: **Proverbs 1**

Hear, my son, your father's instruction,
And reject not your mother's teaching. Proverbs 1:8 RSV

In studying the first chapter of Proverbs this morning it was impressed upon my spirit to share what I am learning. To gain a clearer understanding of the Proverbs, one must study the historical context of how they were written and preserved. For instance, King Solomon has been credited for writing the proverbs, however, there are other writers who may have contributed as well. Our knowledge of Solomon from other portions of scripture helps us to situate proverbs in a context and be able to gain a deeper understanding of their meaning.

Beginning with the first chapter of Proverbs, we are introduced to a comparison of the wise man and the fool. Verses 1-7 are exceptionally applicable for our lives today. This prologue sets the tone for anyone who wants to live in God's way. Our lives will be defined by whether we choose to be the wise man or the fool. Solomon makes it clear that wisdom begins with a fear of the Lord.

Wisdom's Call is the topic in verses 20-33. These are a rebuke to those who choose not to follow God's call for wisdom. The first chapter ends with a simple statement of our call and hope as Christians: "but he who listens to me will dwell securely and will be at ease, without dread of evil." Those who listen and fear the Lord will grow in knowledge and wisdom.

PRAYER FOCUS:
True wisdom is from God and God alone.

PRAYER:
*Father God, may we remember to seek Your wisdom
in our decisions and choices today.*

THOUGHT FOR THE DAY:
*What we choose to do each day depends on many things, but
the most important thing we are guided by is God's wisdom.*

THE GOD WHO LOVES

READ: Psalm 36

O, continue thy steadfast love to those who know thee,
And thy salvation to the upright of heart! Psalm 36:10 RSV

When I think of the many facets of God's love, the most precious gift is His love for mankind, namely that He sent his only son, Jesus Christ, to live on this earth, minister, die, and be resurrected. This unprecedented love means that one day we will be with Him in heavenly places, along with our loved ones that have gone on before us.

This is the ultimate love that God has for us as human beings. Knowing this, I seek God's love so that it transcends other areas in my life, through devotionals and personal interactions with people. In reading Psalm 36, we begin to understand God's unconditional love that helps us in our burdens and pains. It also helps us understand such important aspects of worship as praising, pleading, wondering, contemplating, complaining, and rejoicing! The Psalter continues in this Psalm to provide an opportunity to further understand our place in worship. God, who loves us, wants us to be authentic and know that we may come to Him with all our pain and all our joy.

PRAYER FOCUS:

Think of those who need to put their trust and
love under the shadow of His wings.

PRAYER:

Father God, Extend your loving-kindness to those who need it, and to those who are seeking it

THOUGHT FOR THE DAY:

How precious is the love of God!

THE GOD WHO SATISFIES

READ: Psalm 104

When you give to them, they gather it up;
When you open your hand,
they are filled with good things. Psalm 104:28 NRSV

Nature is truly God's gift: the summer flowers that have turned into the fall colors, a park that autumn has turned into a fairyland with reds, oranges, and tree-fields smothered in burnished gold. Scenes that delight one's senses and make me ever aware of how God is in everything and is everything. For this I am grateful and give Him the praise.

We think of how the material things of the world do not satisfy our souls and we have a void if we continually seek those things. It is the things of God that satisfy, the spiritual things that only God can give that satisfy that 'hole' in one's heart. Once God is our first love, all these other worldly things will dim and become less desirable. It is in serving people, recognizing God's kingdom at work, and working with God in his creation that brings satisfaction in our lives.

PRAYER FOCUS:
People in our world need God and Christ Jesus as their first love.

PRAYER:
Father God, You alone are our heart's desire,
and we long to worship you.

THOUGHT FOR THE DAY:
In what ways can I seek God this day and
let the worldly desires fall away?

THE GOD WHO RESTORES

READ: **Psalm 30**

Sing praises to the Lord,
O you his faithful ones,
And give thanks to his holy name.
For his anger is but for a moment,
his favor is for a lifetime.
Weeping may linger for the night,
But joy comes with the morning. Psalm 30:4-6 NRSV

God allows our lives to be challenged by trials and tribulations. In so doing, we grow spiritually, and if we have the right attitude, then we can be formed both in our hard times and good. The key is remaining faithful in our prayer life, our Bible study, meditations, journaling, going to church, and remaining in community with His people.

I have faced many health issues in my life and looking back, I see it as affirmation of God's work in my life. Although doubts would creep in at the most difficult times, it was a process of being compliant and obedient to professional care. Through the blessing of a kind, loving and supportive family and church family and friends, I can look back and say that God has truly restored my health and well-being.

PRAYER FOCUS:
Though life may present us with hardship, God
is faithful to restore if we are willing.

PRAYER:

Father God, we give you praise with thanksgiving for the hard times in our lives, knowing that we are being strengthened for Your purposes and future plans. Rather than become discouraged and downhearted, let us rest in you, knowing that in your time, our lives will be restored to even greater glory for the ongoing work of Your kingdom. Amen.

THOUGHT FOR THE DAY:

God is waiting for us to call upon Him in our troubles.

GOD AWAITS YOUR PRAISE

READ: **Psalm 147**

Great is our Lord, and abundant in power;
His understanding is beyond measure. Psalm 147:5 RSV

Are there things in your life right now that make you feel anxious or depressed? What is giving you hope? Psalm 147 is a psalm of pure praise. If you read the entire psalm and read it as a prayer, it will become your prayer of praise to the Lord. He wants our praise as we begin each prayer. If it seems hard to begin a prayer with praise, then let God's word guide you through psalms such as this. God understands your every need and as our creator and sustainer, we must praise Him continually. In our worship services, we sing hymns of praise to our God and this can lift our hearts and souls above the mundane things of our lives to a much higher plane that only God can give. He is waiting for your praises to Him this day.

PRAYER FOCUS:
God, who understands us better than we understand
ourselves, is waiting for us to offer our praises to Him.

PRAYER:
Father God, We praise you as our infinite loving God who
accepts us and wants our praise in all things. Amen

THOUGHT FOR THE DAY:
For those who want to praise the Lord, let
them seek out the Psalms of Praise.

THE GOD WHO LISTENS

READ: Psalm 34

The eyes of the Lord are on the righteous,
And His ears are attentive to their cry. Psalm 34:15 NIV

Psalm 34 is unique in its insistence on praising and blessing God at all times. When the Psalmist sought the Lord, he heard him and this is a truth we can claim today as well. God also delivered David from his fears. David cried out and God listened and he was saved from his troubles.

God's eyes are on the righteous and His ears are attentive to their cries. God's face is against those who do evil, and they will be cut off from His remembrance. The Lord hears the cries of the righteous and delivers them out of all their troubles. The Lord is near to those with a broken heart, and saves them with a contrite spirit. The Lord redeems the soul of His servants and none of those who trust in Him shall be condemned.

PRAYER FOCUS:
God's relationship with us depends upon our willingness
to call on Him, for He is always near and wanting
to help in whatever we are going through.

PRAYER:
Father God, we claim this Psalm today and ask that it
become resting place as we go through various trials.

THOUGHT FOR TODAY:
Be an open ear to someone who needs to experience God's love today.

9

TRAIN UP A CHILD

READ: Proverbs 22

Train up a child in the way he should go,
And when he is old he will not depart from it. Proverbs 22:6 RSV

I'm reminded of a time when a dear friend came to visit our home and brought along her eight-year-old son. It was a lively time with an inquisitive child who soaked up new information like a sponge. It was a joy to see this young one, so tender in age, be guided by his patient mother as she wove into their conversations the things that she wished to teach him. As we watched, this young boy explored the backyard and garden. He collected flower blossoms, leaves, and other parts of nature always wanting to know their name.

My friend, the mother of this child, had found ways to channel his energy into a learning experience for everything. I was amazed at how well she understood her child and had a wonderful way of talking to him. He had been taught good manners and exercised them in our home. He is taken to church and Sunday school regularly.

That visit will be a memory of delight as I think of the gift God has entrusted to my friend with this young child. We can be assured, as in Proverbs 22:6, that training a child in the way he/ she should go and when they are old they will not depart from it.

PRAYER FOCUS:
OUR CHILDREN.

PRAYER:

Dear Father, thank you for the lives of children who are taught the way they should go by loving and committed parents. Help us to love the little children as you do.

THOUGHT FOR THE DAY:

Our children grow up quickly in today's world. Let us take every opportunity to train them up in the way they should go.

CONSTANT COMPANIONS

READ: **Proverbs 12**

The righteous know the needs of their animals,
But the mercy of the wicked is cruel. Proverbs 12:10 NRSV

Sunshine, our faithful and loving cat, is my constant companion. One day, I went to the local animal shelter and there, behind a glass wall, in a shoebox, was Sunshine. She was five months old and a thin, but bright-eyed kitten. I sat down and she came right to me, raised up on her hind legs, placed her paws on my leg, and looked into my eyes, as if saying "Take me home." I was smitten! She won my heart and has grown to be a wonderful companion over the years.

One thing that we noticed in those early days with Sunshine was that she didn't like to be held in our laps. She will only get close when I am feeling ill and resting on the couch. She will jump up on the back of the couch with one paw hanging close to me. It's as if she is saying, "I sense something is not right with you, and I care."

My hope is that people who read this that are alone may know that God created us for relationship. Joy can be found in the companionship of pets as well as those around us. We are relational people and need to be in relationships that help us grow.

PRAYER FOCUS:

May we see be more aware of people in need of companionship.

PRAYER:

Father God, thank you for the world You created here on earth for our care, love, and protection. May we regard all of your creation as precious, as we are taught in Proverbs 12:10.

THOUGHT FOR THE DAY:

How would a pet help your life? If you already have a pet, think of it as God's special gift to you and a blessing of companionship.

THE FRUIT OF THE SPIRIT

READ: Galatians 5:22-23

*But the fruit of the Spirit is love, joy, peace, forbearance,
kindness, goodness, faithfulness, gentles, and self-control.
Against such things there is now law.*
Galatians 5:22-23 NIV

Each morning, I end my devotional by asking God to instill the Fruit of the Spirit in me as I go about the day. Let us dwell on them for a moment.

Love, Joy, and Peace: These three naturally go together and are easy to remember. Love, the most important, must exist in our relationship to God and to others. Joy and peace happen as an outpouring of love. These are essential to an abundant life in Christ. Ask God to help you remember these throughout your day.

Forbearance, Kindness, and Goodness: These follow in a natural sequence. Isn't it wonderful to meet a person with genuine kindness and goodness toward others? Have you known a truly patient person? These each contain a unique yet still essential characteristic of the faithful Christian we are called to be. Ask God to help you remember these throughout your day.

Faithfulness, Gentleness, and Self-control: Faithfulness is what God calls us to as we believe in the Christian message of resurrection and hope of new life. The Christian life then is tempered by gentleness and self-control to keep our emotions, and our words, in check, no matter what happens to us each day. Ask God to help you remember these throughout your day.

PRAYER FOCUS:

May we remember the Fruit of the Spirit in each moment of the day.

PRAYER:

Father God, Thank you for your Fruit of the Spirit, may we think and pray about them each day, asking for each one.

THOUGHT FOR THE DAY:

Consider your day with the Fruit of the Spirit, compared to a day without the Fruit of the Spirit?

TENDING GARDENS

———

READ: Genesis 2

And the Lord God planted a garden in Eden, in the east; and there
he put the man whom he had formed. Genesis 2:8 NRSV

Gardening has always been of special interest to me growing up in the arid desert of West Texas. My dad taught me the basics of vegetable gardening and my grandmother taught me the love and appreciation of flowers. Learning and working in a garden, gives us a new appreciation for God's creation.

In God's Word there are countless stories of God's gardens, the act of gardening, and their importance for survival, comfort, protection, and pleasure. In Genesis, God created the Garden of Eden. It was a garden made by God for Adam and Eve to live and survive with ease. It was sufficient for their existence. Although the story may not end in the garden, it is significant that the place where humanities' relationship with God began is in the garden. This is the place God chose to build relationship with us.

The garden in our backyard remains one of bounty and beauty. It brings joy to share our surplus with friends, family, neighbors, and even the birds. Working and harvesting this garden has been a blessing to us and the people in our community. We share our harvest with local food kitchens that desperately need fresh, organically grown local produce. Tending a well-grown garden brings blessings to others, as we know that God blesses us, as we serve Him. As we work in the garden, the place where God first walked with humanity, we remember God's desire to be in relationship with all of us.

PRAYER FOCUS:

Remember those who are less fortunate than you. How can you be a blessing to someone this week?

PRAYER:

Father God, We give you and only you the praise and honor for the fruitful gardens of our lives, so that we may share with others. Amen.

THOUGHT FOR THE DAY:

How well do we tend our gardens that God has given us?

THE FRUITFUL OLD PEAR TREE

READ: **Matthew 7**

So, every sound tree bears good fruit, but the bad tree bears evil fruit.
Matthew 7:17 RSV

Every August, our Orient Pear of twenty-plus years begins to drop her fruit of delicious and wonderfully formed pears, hundreds of them. I constantly hear thuds on the grass. Another ripe pear has fallen to the ground. It is ready to be given away to our waiting list of friends and family and neighbors. It is indeed a blessing to share our bountiful crop each year. We are blessed as we bless others. And yet, for as many pears that were picked for good fruit, at least as many or more, were thrown into the compost pile as bad fruit.

As we turn to Matthew 7, we are reminded of the both the good and bad fruit. Our lives, in this parable, are known by the fruit we leave behind. Our legacy is our fruit. Will you leave good fruit or bad? What will your legacy be?

PRAYER FOCUS:
*God desires for us to produce good fruit. May we have
eyes to see and ears to hear where God is leading.*

PRAYER:
*Father God, we want to always honor and please you with the good
fruits of our lives, the first fruits, and cast away bad fruit coming from
false teachers. Help, O Lord Jesus to know the difference. Amen.*

THOUGHT FOR THE DAY:
God is honored and pleased with our good fruits.

DEVOTIONAL FOR MOTHER'S DAY

READ: John 19:17-30

Near the cross of Jesus stood his mother, his mother's sister, Mary the
wife of Clopas, and Mary Magdalene. When Jesus saw his mother
there, and the disciple whom he loved standing nearby, he said to
her, :Woman, here is your son," and to the disciple, "Here is your
mother." From that time on, this disciple took her into his home.
John 19:25-27 NIV

As you are well aware, this Sunday is recognized as Mother's Day. The commercials are pounding out the message: "Go out and buy her flowers and gifts!"; "Always call your mothers!" Many of you have lost your mothers and have lasting memories of the days she cared for you. Many out there do not have the perfect, storybook relationship with their mother. While others have good relationships and are grateful.

I am blessed to have my mother still living. She will be celebrating her 80th birthday next week. Her daughters, myself, the eldest, will be traveling to see her and our step-dad and spend the weekend. Despite some major health issues, my mother is alert. She lives for the moments when her children and grandchildren come to visit her. She is a godly woman and always ends our telephone conversations saying, "I am praying for you."

In reading the scriptures this morning, I was blessed to read again the story where Jesus provides for His mother. Even on the cross, moments before his death, in agony, Jesus was concerned about His mother and her well-being. He made sure that one of his disciples would care for her and take her to his home. May we all take Jesus' example to heart.

PRAYER FOCUS:

Mothers around the world caring for children
who need support themselves.

PRAYER:

Dear Father,
Let us honor our mothers in special ways if they are still with us. Let
us honor our mother's memory if she has gone to be with You. Let us
remember the example of Jesus Christ, honoring and remembering
His mother, even to death. In His holy and precious name, Amen.

THOUGHT FOR THE DAY:

How can we follow in the example of Jesus by
caring and giving support to our mothers?

PRAYER OF JABEZ

READ: 1 Chronicles 4

Jabez called on the God of Israel, saying "Oh that you would bless me and enlarge my border, and that your hand might be with me, and that you would keep me from hurt and harm!" 1 Chronicles 4:10 NRSV

Yesterday, I was reminded of the Prayer of Jabez as I dialogued with a friend about wanting the Prayer of Jabez for her loved one's memorial stone. I had never thought of writing that short prayer on a tombstone, but what a wonderful concept and lasting legacy for those who will see this monument for years to come.

There are many people in our lives that are literally consumed with emotional pain and suffering. I pray that this prayer will bring hope and peace for those who are feeling hopeless. When we feel weak and hopeless is when God is more able to touch our lives with His saving grace to restore our souls.

PRAYER FOCUS:
For those who may experience fear and pain, that they may find comfort in these words.

PRAYER:
Dear Father,
I lift up those who need the "Prayer of Jabez." God, may you bless them, enlarge their territory, let your hand be with them, and keep them from harm so that they will be free of pain. Please grant their request. Amen.

THOUGHT FOR TODAY:
May we find ways to offer the pleas of the Prayer of Jabez to the people around us this week.

21

RENEWAL FOR SPRINGTIME

READ: **Psalm 103**

Bless the Lord, O my soul; and all that is within me, bless his holy name!
Bless the Lord, O my soul, and forget not all his benefits,
Who forgives all you iniquity, who heals all your diseases,
Who redeems your life from the pit, who crowns
you with steadfast love and mercy,
Who satisfies you with good as long as you live,
So that your youth is renewed like the eagle's. Psalm 103:4-5 RSV

I've taken a couple of weeks off for spring break and a trip to Southern California to visit our son, our daughter-in-law, and grandsons. The boys were on spring break during Easter week. My husband went this time and we had a wonderful, blessed time with these special people in our lives. Southern California is beautiful this time of year with it's lush tropical landscapes. Only God's paintbrush could create such lingering beauty to the eye...as far as you look there is something breathtakingly new to awe in God's glory.

We spent quality time with our grandsons each day, playing hours of basketball with their granddad in the front yard, a day trip to the mountains, board games in the evenings, going to their church, sitting outside on the sunny days by the pool for me, writing future devotionals and reading two new books, and so much more. Experiencing family in the midst of God's beautiful creation can only inspire praise and worship.

PRAYER FOCUS:
It is good to have times of renewal and love in our
lives, especially when family is so far apart.

PRAYER:

Dear Father,
In our busy lives in which the days, weeks, months, and
years go by so quickly, let us make time and take the time
for the people dearest to us, our family. May we be ever
mindful that these times are lasting...even into eternity.
In Jesus name, Amen.

THOUGHT FOR TODAY:

Who can I call in my family today to let them know
someone loves them and cares for them?

JOY

———

READ: **Psalm 43**

Then I will go to the altar of God,
To God my exceeding joy;
And I will praise thee with the lyre,
O God, my God.
Why are you cast down, O my soul,
And why are you disquieted with me?
Hope in God; for I shall again praise him,
My help and my God. Psalm 43:4-5 RSV

This morning I was seeking out scriptures for 'Joy' and how to have joy amid the crises, storms, and perplexities of life. God's people need the joy of their salvation renewed in the Lord Jesus Christ. What a wonderful way to begin the day by reading the psalms each morning before the day begins. We find in Psalms like Psalm 43 the reason for our Joy. We can take refuge in God. God need not go on mourning. When we realize these truths. The Psalter tells us we should go to altar of God, so that we may praise God. We take comfort and find joy in the Psalters affirmation of God's work and glory.

PRAYER FOCUS:
May we be constantly reminded that God is in control.

PRAYER:
Dear Father,
Hear our prayer amid the turmoil, unrest, and storms of life,
to find our hope and joy in Jesus, our redeemer, savior and
friend. In His precious name, humbly we pray, Amen.

God is our defender, our refuge, our light, our help, our joy! Share these truths with those you see today.

REST AND RELAX

READ: **Proverbs 3**

Trust in the Lord with all your heart
and lean not on your own understanding;
in all your ways submit to him,
and he will make your paths straight.
Proverbs 3: 5-6 NIV

This is the day to make time for resting and relaxing. God wants you to "float awhile" and regain your strength. How many times do we start to rest and something comes up and takes us away into whatever has called our name? Resting and relaxing in the Lord is essential for our mental well-being and our physical healing. My prayer is that as you read this today, you will devote time for yourself and rest in the Lord. We all have the exact same amount of time each day, it is how you use it and prioritize it!

PRAYER FOCUS:
Don't be afraid to just sit in the quiet. Allow God to speak in the moments of quiet.

PRAYER:
Dear Father,
God, We praise you for the rest and relaxation that is given when
we seek you through prayer, rest, and meditation upon Your word.
In Jesus name, Amen.

THOUGHT FOR TODAY:
We all need moments of rest and relaxation. Find short
moments in your day to say a little prayer and be renewed.

A WAY OF ESCAPE

READ: Psalm 124

We have escaped like a bird
From the snare of the fowlers;
The snare is broken,
And we have escaped! Psalm 124:7 NRSV

One afternoon, late in the day, I heard the noisy chirping of a frantic bird that was trapped in our greenhouse! It had flown in through the overhead air vent and was caught in a snare. The sun was setting and I couldn't locate the bird and knew it would probably be morning before it could see the light of day and escape. The next morning, sure as the sun rises in the East, this little creature had started its nervous chirping and flying about in search of escape. I spotted it and identified it as a male house wren, tiny, dark brown, with a long sharp beak, and long tail.

I opened the overhead air vents and prayed that my little friend would find his way out. I went on about my daily tasks, trusting God to take care of the situation. Surely as the sun sets in the West, Mister Wren found the way to freedom and escape. I felt a sense of relief and thankfulness.

How many times do we become "trapped" in situations of life and don't know the way of escape? Do we trust God to rescue us from the snares of our lives? Are we willing to let God deliver us? Just as the little wren escaped from his snare, we can as well. *Our help is in the name of the Lord, who made heaven and earth.* Psalm 124:8 NRSV

PRAYER FOCUS:

From the rising to the setting of the sun,
God is a constant presence in our lives.

PRAYER:

Dear Father,
Thank you for the metaphor used in the scripture today of the
snares of life. When we are feeling trapped, let us find the way of
escape through prayer and trusting deliverance in your time.
In Jesus name, Amen.

THOUGHT FOR THE DAY:

What area of my life have I not fully trusted into God's hands?

GODLY WISDOM

READ: Proverbs 4

Get wisdom, get understanding; do not forget
my words or turn away from them.
Do no forsake wisdom, and she will protect you.
The beginning of wisdom is this: Get wisdom.
Though it cost all you have, get understanding.
Cherish her, and she will exalt you; embrace her, and she will honor you.
She will give you a garland to grace your head and present
you with a glorious crown. Proverbs 4:5-9 NIV

I visited an elderly friend recently and came away blessed with her wisdom. This wonderful Christian lady came into my life almost two years ago. I have gotten to know this special person through our one-on-one visits in her home, visits to her doctors, emails back and forth, phone calls, sharing prayer requests, candy making classes in her home, discussions of the Bible and her faith, and so much more. Of all the remarkable qualities in my friend's life that have been imparted to me it is her Godly wisdom that is a gift from God. She has blessed my life beyond measure and I thank God for this rich gift of friendship, a lifelong friendship.

I believe that all wisdom comes from God. Desiring to be wise in the eyes of God is what we should strive for each day of our lives. Worldly wisdom is short-lived and dissipates in a moment. Godly wisdom is solid, secure, and eternal. This type of wisdom makes our lives rich here on this earth. We take Godly wisdom with us into our eternal lives with Jesus Christ and God. May God continue to bless you with this precious gift of His wisdom that you have been given to bless others along your way!

PRAYER FOCUS:

May God open our ears and our eyes and close our mouths so we may learn from His wisdom.

PRAYER:

Dear Father,
Today as we go about our daily routines of mundane things, we pray for Godly wisdom in our thoughts, words, and deeds. Let us get wisdom and understanding from your ways, scriptures, and from the people in our lives who have the gift of wisdom.
In Jesus name, Amen.

THOUGHT FOR TODAY:

Who are the "wise" people in your life and how can you be more attentive to them?

THE OLD PEAR TREE

READ: **Psalm 1**

But his delight is in the law of the Lord,
And on his law he meditates day and night.
He is like a tree planted by streams of water,
That yields its fruit in its season, and its leaf does not wither.
In all that he does, he prospers. Psalm 1:2-3 RSV

I reclined in our patio swing and enjoyed watching the bees at work on the thousands of snowy white blooms that cover the old pear tree. The bees appeared to know exactly where they were to go, pollinating the flowers, and extracting nectar for making their honey. There was a beautiful harmony to their busy work.

In the autumn, delicious pears will grace our dinner table, along with pear butter, pear pies, pear preserves, and the joy of sharing these treats with friends! I thought, as I watched this process, how wonderfully God made this pear tree that blooms at springtime -- knowing its purpose along with the bees knowing theirs. There is no toiling or strife, just the natural flow and rhythm of the cycle of nature that God put into place. I pondered -- how it would be if we, as God's highest creation, could find our place in the scheme of things so easily?

Many people strive all their lives, searching for God's exact purpose. Do we look in the right places? If we are seeking those answers in worldly pursuits, we will not find them. We have the Holy Scriptures, Godly people of influence, and the Holy Spirit to guide us and show us His purpose for our lives. God speaks to us through the life cycle of old pears trees in our lives. If God speaks to us through these small movements in his kingdom, think what greater work he has in stored for us if we are able to open our eyes to see his full Kingdom at work.

PRAYER FOCUS:

How can be more attentive to God's Kingdom at work around me?

PRAYER:

Dear Father,
Thank you for your truths revealed to us in the wonder of nature.
Thank you for the promise of life eternal through the plan of
salvation through Jesus Christ. Thank you for showing and revealing
Your purpose for our lives through the divine plan of nature. Let
us reflect upon these promises as we meditate day and night.
In Jesus name, Amen.

THOUGHT FOR TODAY:

Take a moment to reflect on God's creation and
work constantly in motion around us.

DEVOTIONAL FOR ASH WEDNESDAY

READ: 1 Corinthians 15:50-59

Listen, I will tell you a mystery! We will not all die, but we will all be changed, in a moment, in the twinkling of an eye, at the last trumpet. For the trumpet will sound, and the dead will be raised imperishable, and we will be changed. 1 Corinthians 15:51-52 NRSV

Today marks the start of Lenten Season. Lenten season is the solemn Christian religious season from Ash Wednesday to Easter, 40 days, kept as a time of fasting and repenting of sins. Some people like to give something up for this time period as a symbol of their devotion to God. However you chose to observe and honor this sacred season is your choice. It is a wonderful time of renewal and redemption, remembering the ultimate sacrifice of Jesus Christ's death on the cross and his resurrection to eternal glory.

PRAYER FOCUS:
May God reveal the parts of our lives from which we need to break away. May God give us the strength to fast from these things and find ourselves deeper in God's spirit.

PRAYER:
Dear Father,
Help us to remember that our lives on this earth are but a mere shadow of the things to come, eternal life through our Lord Jesus Christ, the reason for Lenten/Easter season. In Jesus holy and precious name.

THOUGHT FOR TODAY:
What act of devotion is God calling you to this week?

33

FOR EVERYTHING THERE IS A SEASON

READ: Ecclesiastes 3:1-8

There is a time for everything,
And a season for every activity under the heavens
Ecclesiastes 3:1 NIV

My beloved brother, a husband, son, father, grandfather, uncle, and friend to many passed to on his eternal glory on December 17, 2005. His battle with pancreatic cancer was gallant, courageous, and strong for nearly a year. God gave me much time with him during this year and I was blessed by his enduring faith and his witness that Jesus Christ was Lord of his life amid his suffering and pain. He knew when he was ready for Hospice and went into it with a joyful spirit. My faith grew stronger as a result of our visits and heart-to-heart talks. I felt he knew that his healing on this earth was not meant to be.

He was laid to rest in a little town in West Texas. It was truly the saddest day of my life, although I know he is with the Lord Jesus, healed, happy, and reunited with his beloved teenage daughter, our daddy, grandparents, and so many more welcoming him into Paradise. I had a comforting dream of him the other night that he was healed, happy, and restored to how he looked before the ravages of cancer destroyed his body. How wonderful is our Lord God to give us dreams of comfort and hope when we are grieving the earthly loss of our dear ones.

A dear friend told me that in our times of grief, defeat, and pain, it is most imperative for us to share our thoughts and feelings with others. If we don't, we leave the door open for the adversary to step in and weaken our faith. By sharing with others what we are going through, our faith is strengthened, and this is what God always asks us to do. We go through hard times to test our faith and always, to help others who are experiencing similar experiences.

PRAYER FOCUS:
May God give us the strength and courage share with those around us.

PRAYER:
God, May we be open to your ways. May we be open to share our struggles. May we be a blessing as we realize how you have blessed us.

THOUGHT FOR TODAY:
May God bless you and bring you peace and comfort with whatever life is offering you right now.

THANKSGIVING

READ: **Psalm 92**

A Psalm. A Song for the Sabbath.
It is good to give thanks to the Lord,
To sing praises to thy name, O Most High;
To declare thy steadfast love in the morning,
And thy faithfulness by night. Psalm 92:1-2 RSV

This Thanksgiving morning, my husband and I volunteered to deliver meals to elderly people in an impoverished area of our city by working for a charity agency that provides these meals on Thanksgiving and Christmas. It was a blessing to see how much these folks appreciated this meal that was provided and delivered to their front doors. Their thanks was profuse. It made us realize our own blessings and to know that it is hard to want 'more' when we saw those with so little, living their lives with a thankful spirit. Their warm smiles and thankful hearts were a joy to behold.

If you want to serve humanity, and understand that it is more of a blessing to give than to receive, I encourage you to sign-up and deliver a Christmas meal to those in need, those in poverty, and those who can no longer work, many who are ill, homebound, and infirmed.

PRAYER FOCUS:
May we seek opportunities to help those who in need

PRAYER:

Father, we thank you for your continued blessings. May we be constantly reminded of our calling to help those around us. May we always be grateful for the gifts you bestow upon us.

THOUGHT FOR TODAY:

How can you serve the Lord by serving others in your community?

WAIT ON THE LORD

READ: **Psalm 27**

The Lord is my light and my salvation; whom shall I fear?
The Lord is the stronghold of my life; of whom shall I be afraid?
When evildoers assail me, uttering slanders against me,
My adversaries and foes, they shall stumble and fall.
Though a host encamp against me, my heart shall not fear;
Though war arise against me, yet I will be confident.
One thing have I asked of the Lord, that will I seek after;
That I may dwell in the house of the Lord all the days of my life,
To behold the beauty of the Lord, and to inquire in his temple.
For he will hide me in his shelter in the day of trouble;
He will conceal me under the cover of his tent,
He will set me high upon a rock. Psalm 27:1-5 RSV

Many of you are going through the valley of the shadow of death with either yourselves or loved ones. These simple verses of scripture are as true today as when they were written thousands of years ago. We need assurance of salvation and I trust these verses will bring that peace to your hearts. Reading the Psalms will bring great comfort. A friend once said that her grandmother read two Psalms and a Proverb everyday for her devotional time with the Lord. If you are searching for a special devotion, this is good advice. God will put those special verses of scripture in your view as you spend time alone in His Word.

PRAYER FOCUS:
Stop for a moment and ask God that you may dwell in his presence

PRAYER:

Dear Father,
Let the meditations of our hearts be acceptable in your sight and let
us find comfort in the reading and meditation on Your Holy Word.

THOUGHT FOR TODAY:

God does not say we will walk through our valleys alone. God is with us.

OFFERING GRACE AND PEACE

READ: I Timothy 5

Honor widows who are really widows. If a widow has children or grandchildren, they should first learn their religious duty to their own family and make some repayment to their parents; for this is please in God's sight. The real widow, left alone, has set her hope on God and continues in supplications and prayers night and day.
I Timothy 5:3-5 NRSV

When a dear friend has recently has become widowed, we must remember this is a difficult time of grieving the loss of her soul mate, and she is adjusting to life on her own. So many unknowns face a person in this situation! It is a time for friends and family to be sensitive and attentive, bringing an unexpected hot meal, a caring card in the mail, an invitation to lunch, a call, an email, a flower or plant, a homemade loaf of bread, a batch of cookies, or best of all, a personal visit, with a listening ear to ease the pain. It's good for the person in grief to be able to weep openly, unashamedly, in the presence of family and friends.

God gave us tears for emotional relief and healing. People in grief want to talk about their departed loved one. It's natural, therapeutic, and healing. Most of all, know that real healing takes time and it varies from person to person. It's good to and not try and 'rush the healing process.' God will guide you as you seek a way to comfort the grieving person. Let the healing begin and let it begin with you and me.

PRAYER FOCUS:
*People who have lost their partners, who are
in need of God's grace and peace.*

PRAYER:
*Dear Father,
Let us comfort the widows, widowers, and all who have recently lost
loved ones. Let us remember that one day we will be facing the same.
Let us have hearts of compassion, just as our Lord Jesus Christ.
In His name, we pray.*

THOUGHT FOR THE DAY:
*In what ways can I seek to honor a widow today,
to embody God's grace and serve a friend?*

A DEAD TREE AND NEW LIFE

READ: **Proverbs 3**

Do not plot harm against your neighbor, who lives trustfully near you.
Proverbs 3:29 NIV

Our next door neighbor's trees along the property line have been dying for several years. They have a way of coming across our wood fence and hanging in our yard. One particular tree had been a source of long term annoyance as it adorned our fence and flower beds. The owner of this tree assured us he would remove the tree, however, the end product was that he left two huge trunks of the dead tree that stand 5 feet above our fence!

We were disappointed that two unsightly huge trunks were left, but then an amazing thing happened! A pair of red-headed woodpeckers took up residence in the dead trunks and hammered away for hours, hollowing out holes for nesting. I began to feel differently about the neighbor's dead tree. We were able to observe first-hand the complete nesting cycle that produced little baby woodpeckers. They are miniatures of their red-headed parents and several days before they fly, they toddle around on the tree trunk and the brick of our house! I watch each morning and evening as the Mother Red sits on her nest, imbedded in the hole, while Father Red sits above on the dead trunk, guarding his precious family. I look forward to the toddlers about to make their debut this year!

What a gift God has given us in the neighbor leaving the dead tree trunks! It is a stark reminder of God's way of working around us. If God can use a dead tree as a lesson of the beauty of new life in His creation, what else is He doing around us in an even bigger way to bring new life?

42

PRAYER FOCUS:

Let us remember that God always has a plan, even if that means patiently waiting for it to be revealed to us.

PRAYER:

Dear Father,

Thank you for our neighbors, even when we are annoyed with them at times. Help us remember to plot no harm against them because they do live trustfully near us.
In Jesus name.

THOUGHT FOR TODAY:

Go and look for God's clever disguises in your neighborhood.

IF AT FIRST YOU DON'T SUCCEED, DON'T TRY AGAIN!

READ: **Proverbs 1**

For in vain is the net baited while the bird.
Proverbs 1:17 NRSV

In this humorous proverb, we can picture the birds aligned along the fence, watching with delight as the farmer covers his grapes with a net. They will quickly perceive where there are gaps, waiting for the right moment to swoop down and eat their fill.

There exists a conflict between instinct and judgment. Birds will respond as birds, making up in persistence what they lack in creative thinking. On the other hand, human beings have been endowed with the ability to examine a situation and make necessary adjustments. To do this, we need to be open to various possibilities and then be willing to change our behavior.

The old motto, "If at first you don't succeed, try, try, again," is not always good advice. Some situations call for an alternative solution. Relationships with loved ones, church programs, our personal health regime---all these and other matters need to be examined from time to time. God constantly puts us in situations where we have the opportunity to learn from our past. The question is whether or not we will choose to do so.

PRAYER FOCUS:
May we be open to the way and the things God is teaching today.

PRAYER:

Dear Father,

We pray for the insight to know when to try, try again or to let go. We pray for wisdom and discernment in our daily decisions and choices. We pray for the knowledge that circumstances may need to be changed with our friends, family, and loved ones. In Jesus name.

THOUGHT FOR TODAY:

Who will God put in our path today to teach us an unexpected lesson? Will we have eyes to see and ears to hear?

HOW WILL GOD USE YOU?

READ: **Romans 12**

So we, though many, are one body in Christ, and individually members of one another. Romans 12:5 RSV

In times when we are struggling with knowing how to serve God and others with our talents and gifts, it is important to remember the happiest and most content people are those who are serving others on a daily basis. They are active in all phases of their lives and know God's plan and purpose for their lives. They do it out of love, not obligation, or a wish for return or reward. It's simply that they love to serve others.

One of my dearest friends has a daily prayer ministry of praying for missionaries far and near, elected officials on the federal, state, and local levels, people in her church and not in her church, her family and friends, and so many more. She gets up long before daybreak, each day, to go through her prayer journal, praying and lifting each one by name to her Lord. She receives many telephone calls each day for new prayer requests. She keeps detailed written accounts of these prayer requests and answers, because she knows her purpose for her life and is using what God gave her the ability and discipline to be a mighty prayer warrior for humanity.

God has given each of us gifts to serve the body of Christ. Whether we serve as a prayer warrior or as a constant servant, it is a part of our calling as the body to find our way of contributing and serving Christ and the church.

PRAYER FOCUS:
May God show us how best we can serve

PRAYER:

Dear Father,
We pray that our gifts and talents, given us, will
be used for Your purpose and Your glory.
In Jesus name.

THOUGHT FOR TODAY:

How can I give of my time and service this day?

A CHILD'S JOY

READ: Mathew 18

At that time the disciples came to Jesus, and asked,
"Who is the greatest in the kingdom of heaven?"
He called a child, whom he put among them, and said,
"Truly, I tell you, unless you change and become like children,
you will never enter the kingdom of heaven.
Whoever becomes humble like this child is the greatest in
the kingdom of heaven." Mathew 18:1-4 NRSV

Once I went on a Wildflower Experimental Garden Tour, and there were several groups of pre-school children taking this tour. They were paired up, holding hands and trailing along behind their teachers. They were allowed to pick one wildflower by the guide when the teachers had previously told them, "Don't pick the flowers!" It was a blessing/joy to see these precious little boys and girls, so beautifully behaved, obeying the instructions of their leaders. Little noses were buried deep in to that single wild flower as they enjoyed the sweet fragrance.

Seeing this tour group of little children reminded me of the joy children bring and reminded me of the sweet presence of Jesus. Along with knowing that God wants each to come to Him, as trusting little children for all our needs, sorrows, pain, grief, and our eternal destiny. And yes, in our times of great joy as in the witnessing of little children on a wildflower tour.

Jesus used a small child to help Him make a point with His Disciples, and to us as well! The point was not to be childish, but rather childlike, with humble and sincere hearts!

PRAYER FOCUS:
May God grant us the faith to come to him as a child

PRAYER:
Father,
May we understand the significance of calling you "Father." We
are truly your children. You are the creator of heaven and earth.
You have given us life. May we come to you recognizing the joy
You have offered us in Christ. For it is in his name we pray,
Amen.

THOUGHT FOR TODAY:
How can we see God in the life of children around us?

THE POWER OF PRAYER

READ: **Mark 2:1-5**

And many were gathered together, so that
there was no longer room for them,
Not even about the door; and he was preaching the word to them.
Mark 2:2 RSV

There was a time our dear friend seemed to grow a bit weaker each day. Cancer had left him emaciated and in constant pain. The doctors who supervised his care were grim about his chances. As his body grew weaker, his faith in God's healing power began to waver and become weak as well.

Then a small group of us began to pray for him. We recalled the four who lowered their crippled friend through a hole in the roof, a hole they had made with their bare hands. Imagine the four carrying their friend to Jesus, only to find they could not get to the healer because of the crowd! Hear the people below complaining as debris begins falling on them from the ever-widening hole appearing in the roof! But see the four refuse to be denied. They persevered until they place the man in front of Jesus. And, scripture tells, Jesus heals the man not because of his faith but because of the faith of his friends.

We realized that we needed to bring our friend into Christ's presence for healing. We began to pray, and God answered. He recovered and soon returned to work.

PRAYER FOCUS:
A friend who is sick.

PRAYER:
*Dear God, help us to be faithful and loving
friends to those who need you. Amen.*

THOUGHT FOR THE DAY:
Whom can I bring to Jesus today?

SPRINGTIME RENEWAL

———

READ: **Solomon 2**

See! The winter is past; the rains are over and gone.
Flowers appear on the earth; the season of singing has come,
The cooing of doves is heard in our land.
Solomon 2:11-12 NIV

Out from the kitchen window I see bright yellow daffodils springing up from the ivy ground cover, a definite sign that spring has come. The trees are beginning to leaf and the countryside is coming alive once more. What a glorious gift from God: the spring season that transforms the dreary winter scene to a spectrum of green from the darkest to the palest shade, and the blossoming of the bulbs from their long winter's nap. It symbolizes how God can change the circumstances in our lives that are gloomy and grey— and seemingly, never-ending; to hope, joy and the anticipation of springtime renewed. It's as if the fog has lifted and the sunshine has returned to our lives.

PRAYER FOCUS:
Remembering love ones lost in the winter of our lives.

PRAYER:
Father,
May we experience the renewal of spring in our hearts and minds.
May we experience the renewal of spring and be reminded of
the resurrection each day. May we find redemption in your gift
of new life. May we find hope in your eternal gift of love.

THOUGHT FOR TODAY:

Find someone to tell about the gift of new life God has offered each of us in Jesus death and resurrection.

LIFE IS A PARADOX

READ: Psalm 22

"He committed his cause to the Lord; let him deliver him,
Let him rescue him, for he delights in him!"
Yet thou are he who took me from the womb;
Thou didst keep me safe upon my mother's breasts.
Upon thee was I cast from my birth,
And since my mother bore me thou has been my God.
Be not far from me, for trouble is near
And there is none to help. Psalms 22:8-11 RSV

In times like these life is a paradox of extremes. Extreme joy and extreme pain that can come almost simultaneously. In one extreme I celebrate the 80th birthday of a dear friend at a party. And at the other end I receive a call with some ominous news about my brother's health. On one hand, it was such joy to be a part of my friend's celebration. He is an outstanding Christian man who has beautifully made his mark on life, and then my joy turned to sadness in a moment, in a split second. It's difficult to imagine how we as finite human beings can have such extreme demands on our emotions even simultaneously.

It can be a great source of comfort and peace to reach out to God in prayer. To pray for his grace and mercy and peace. When the pendulum swings from one end to another, and we find ourselves at the mercy of the unknown we must remember to keep God close. God wants us to pray for others in their troubles and in their joys.

PRAYER FOCUS:
Lift up the joys and struggles of life to God.

PRAYER:

God,

We are made aware each and every day of the fragility of life. We don't just laugh with those who laugh and we don't just cry with those who cry. We are often the one laughing, the one crying. Give us peace in those moments of extreme emotional strain. As we suffer, may we recognize that it was your Son who suffered for us. It is your Son who continues to suffer with us. Yet, in the midst of that suffering, we are offered a hope of healing for Jesus's story did not end in the tomb and neither does ours.

THOUGHT FOR TODAY:

Find a moment to be still and listen as God speaks.

TRUE GIFT OF CHRISTMAS

READ: James 1

Every generous act of giving, with every perfect gift, is
from above, coming down from the Father of lights, with
whom there is no variation or shadow due to change.
James 1:17 NRSV

For some, Christmas is a joyous time, and for others it can be a sad time. Whatever the feelings you may have at this time of the year, we can be assured that the gift of eternal life through Christ Jesus can't be taken away...and we rejoice in this truth, in the Christmas season.

The first Christmas was announced by an angel: "I bring you good news of great joy for everyone." We must be thankful for those words that ring true this Christmas season. We must be thankful for the gift of His son, Jesus—

The ultimate gift of love for humankind! God cares about us and what happens in our lives and we are called to help share this love with others along the way.

When you are planning your gathering of family and friends... consider setting aside a time of fellowship and take turns really listening to each other. Some things to ask are: What were you most thankful for this past year? What have you learned from the past year? How would you like to grow in the next year?

PRAYER FOCUS:
Thank God for the gift of Jesus.

PRAYER:

Lord, help us never to take for granted the gifts of life and eternal life that you have given us. In Jesus name.

THOUGHT FOR TODAY:

How can I express my thankfulness for the gift God has given to me today?

MARY AND MARTHA

READ: Luke 10

Now as they went on their way, he entered a village;
And a woman named Martha received him into her house.
And she had a sister called Mary,
Who sat at the Lord's feet and listened to his teaching.
But Martha was distracted with much serving;
And she went to him and said,
"Lord, do you not care that my sister has left me to serve alone?
Tell her then to help me." But the Lord answered her,
"Martha, Martha, you are anxious and troubled about many things;
one thing is needful. Mary has chosen the good portion,
which shall not be taken away from her." Luke 10:38-42 RSV

Many of us are "Marthas". We can see something of ourselves in this conflict between two sisters. One person ends up doing all the work while the others have fun visiting and celebrating another Christmas season. It has become tradition to have parties during this time of year, to rejoice in Christian fellowship. And in the midst of these parties when the hosting duties overwhelm our attention we must not forget to be the "Mary" and enjoy our guests. My prayer is that each one of us can become the "Mary" in the story and know that we have chosen Jesus and he won't be taken away from us.

PRAYER FOCUS:
Be still

PRAYER:

Dear Father, we thank you for the Martha's and Mary's of this world. We need both, but at this season of celebrating your birth once more, let us choose what is better, like Mary and know that you are first and foremost in our lives. In Jesus name, Amen.

THOUGHT FOR TODAY:

Do I need to be a Martha or a Mary today?

MAKING CONNECTIONS

READ: **Psalms 143**

Let the morning bring me word of your unfailing love,
For I have put my trust in you.
Show me the way I should go, for to you I entrust my life.
Psalm 143:8 NIV

In an age of such effortless technological dependence, all it takes is a simple problem to knock you off balance. One small detail can unhinge a daily routine such as morning bible study. Maybe it's a faulty internet connection, a device with no charge, a malfunctioning component, some missing link that causes an interruption to our connection with technology. Sometimes you can run circles around solving the problem, you can test one thing and then another, or be told that the problem is caused by one error only to turn around and be told something completely different. Frustration begins to build and then, when your patience is stretched beyond its limit, the solution reveals itself. And whether the solution is simple or complicated, whether it was user error or mechanical failure, the connection is restored.

With God, unlike technological issues, our connection is always immediate. There are no complicated steps, and no technician is required to reestablish our link. And if we are willing to connect with God, then God is always right there, ready and willing to connect to us. To hear our prayers and our problems.

PRAYER FOCUS:
Let my connection to God be constant. Let
my reliance on him be effortless.

PRAYER:

*Dear Father, as the psalmist wrote,
"Let me hear in the morning of thy steadfast love,
For in thee I put my trust. Teach me the way I should go, for to thee
I lift up my soul." Let me know that even when life gets frustrating
or hectic, You are still there with us. In Jesus name, amen.*

THOUGHT FOR TODAY:

*May I not allow the distractions of the world keep me
from recognizing God's presence around me.*

SEASONS OF CHANGE

READ: Ecclesiastes 3:1-8

For everything there is a season,
and a time for every matter under heaven:
A time to be born, and a time to die;
A time to plant, and a time to pluck up what is planted.
Ecclesiastes 3:1-2 NRSV

The changing seasons can often be a time of great reflection. At the time of year when summer fades into autumn I am faced with the dilemma of when to pluck up beautiful pink and white begonias in my garden. I know that in a short time, the evening temperatures will fall and the begonias will be gone! The scriptures remind me that the seasons have been established by God along with the patterns of life and death. I cannot save the begonias when it is time for them to die, but I find real joy in knowing that their beauty was but for a season. And the season has changed, calling for a new flower that will bloom all winter long and remind me that God works in our lives to bring forth beauty in every season.

PRAYER FOCUS:
What season are you in?

PRAYER:
Dear Father,
Help us to see the beauty in every season of our lives as in
the cycle of the flowering seasonal plants. Let us give thanks
for the changing seasons and the beauty of each flower
that grows for your glory. In Jesus' name. Amen.

THOUGHT FOR TODAY:
Is God causing a season of change in your life? How will you respond?

FINDING STRENGTH IN GOD

READ: Isaiah 40

Have you not known? Have you not heard?
The Lord is the everlasting God,
The Creator of the ends of the earth.
He does not faint or grow weary,
His understanding is unsearchable.
He gives power to the faint,
And to him who has no might he increases strength,
They shall mount up with wings like eagles,
They shall run and not be weary,
They shall walk and not faint. Isaiah 40:28-31 RSV

We all face time in our lives that require supernatural strength from God. Maybe our health has taken uncertain turns, our finances have yielded unpredictable demands. What is impossible for us is always possible with God. How many times do we really acknowledge this truth in our struggles? God is ready to help us. All we have to do is ask with a humble heart and willing spirit and have faith that he will hear us when we are defeated and fill us with his grace so that we shall walk and not faint.

PRAYER FOCUS:
Help us find our strength in God.

PRAYER:

Dear Father,
Help those today who are struggling with overwhelming
circumstances to lean on the promises of Isaiah for
assurance and peace. In Jesus' name. Amen.

THOUGHT FOR TODAY:

Remember that God is with you in moments of weakness

FATHER GOD, THE GARDENER

READ: John 15

"I am the true vine, and my Father is the gardener. He cuts off every branch in me that bears no fruit, while every branch that does bear fruit he prunes so that it will be even more fruitful. You are already clean because of the word I have spoken to you. Remain in me, as I also remain in you. No branch can bear fruit by itself; it must remain in the vine. Neither can you bear fruit unless you remain in me. I am the vine; you are the branches. If you remain in me and I in you, you will bear much fruit; apart from me you can do nothing. John 15:1-5 NIV

How many times do we set out to do things in life on our own without first seeking the Lord's guidance and blessing? If we really believe that Jesus Christ is the true vine and the Father God is the gardener, then we are called to bear fruit. Jesus speaks, in the verses above, of pruning the fruit as it bears fruit. The process of pruning is God's shaping us as we pursue his purposes. Just as we are promised to be shaped as we bear fruit, in the same manner God promises to cut those off who are not bearing fruit. We must strive to be those who honor God and God will honor our service.

I encourage you to start this day with a quiet time of prayer, reading scripture, and relying completely on the Lord for the end result.

PRAYER FOCUS:

How can I best serve God?

Dear Father, I thank you and praise you that your truth is found in these scriptures today. As we make each decision that will impact ourselves and others, let us look to you as the master gardener of our lives. Let us be willing to be pruned so that we may be even more fruitful for your purpose and glory. In Jesus' name. Amen

THOUGHT FOR TODAY:

How can I bear fruit for God today?

ANXIOUS FOR NOTHING

READ: Philippians 4

Do not worry about anything, but in everything by prayer and
supplication with thanksgiving let your requests be made known
to God. And the peace of God, which surpasses all understanding,
will guard your hearts and your minds in Jesus Christ.
Philippians 4:6-7 NRSV

There are times in our lives when it seems like all we can do is worry. Anxiety has become so prevalent that it permeates every area of our lives. It can manifest in anyone, despite their triumphs and successes, worry and apprehension remain a part of the human condition. We must remember that when anxiety overwhelms us, Paul tells us that it is in those moments that we should go to God in prayer. The scriptures call for us to seek him with *thanksgiving*, and know that he will give us peace. It is the peace of God that will keep our hearts and our minds in Christ. We should take hope and comfort in the words of Paul. Anxiety is not a final state for us but a state that should move us to the peace of God.

PRAYER FOCUS:
Give us your peace in the midst of our anxiety

PRAYER:
Dear Father, let us cast our burdens on you, knowing you will sustain
us with the peace that transcends anxiety. In Jesus' name. Amen.

THOUGHT FOR TODAY:
God's peace is greater than any worry

BLESSED GRANDCHILDREN

READ: Psalms 118

This is the day that the Lord has made;
Let us rejoice and be glad in it. Psalm 118:24 NRSV

A visit from our grandsons proved revitalizing for my mind and spirit. And we must rise to sing praises and gives thanks to the Lord God for such good gifts. Having children with us lets us relive the times our sons were home, delighting in childhood play and time spent fishing. One thing we encouraged them to do during their stay was learn the Ten Commandments by heart. How amazing it was to see how quickly they learned each one, in order, by number. Now they will have them in their hearts forever! I challenge you to find a few verses that are special to you and commit them to memory. They will encourage you in unexpected ways as you go about your day.

PRAYER FOCUS:
Pray for your children and/or grandchildren

PRAYER:
Father, Grant us a passion for your word. Enliven us with
your joy, the joy of a child. Remind us of your word as
we go about our day. In your name we pray, Amen

THOUGHT FOR TODAY:
What verses are significant to you? Find those
and commit them to memory

FREEDOM

READ John 8

So if the Son sets you free, you will be free indeed.
John 8:36 NIV

There are so many reasons to celebrate the fourth of July. It is a time to give thanks for our country's freedom and to honor the military that protects it. Many tears are shed around this time of year as we honor those gave their lives for our precious freedom. Tears of grief for those lost and tears of joy, knowing that God is still supreme in our country. We know that is Christ Jesus who is truly supreme and gives us our ultimate freedom. In that knowledge and truth we are free. And at times when we express our gratitude and pride that we live in a country where we can freely claim our savior, we must remember those in other countries who do not have that ability. We must pray that God's word reaches beyond our borders to touch those who need freedom the most.

PRAYER FOCUS:
Those living in situations where they are not free to religious expression

PRAYER:
Dear Father,
Thank you for all our precious freedoms but especially our freedom
to worship. Let us remember and honor those men and women who
have given their lives for this freedom. Let us remember those who are
serving our country in areas of combat, who stand in harm's way at
this very moment. We pray that you protect them wherever they are.

We pray for our leaders and the leaders of all countries. We pray for an end to war. Let us always remember that only in Christ are we free. Free from the perils of sin and destruction. In Jesus' name. Amen.

THOUGHT FOR TODAY:

Thank someone who has served and sacrificed for our freedom

THE BLESSING OF CHILDREN

READ: Psalm 128

Blessed are all who fear the Lord, who walk in obedience to him.
You will eat the fruit of your labor; blessings and prosperity will be yours.
Your wife will be like a fruitful vine within your house;
Your children will be like olive shoots around your table.
Yes, this will be the blessing for the man who fears the Lord.
Psalm 128:1-4 NIV

Many of us know the blessing of children and the double blessing of grandchildren. Visits with our children and grandchildren can revive our souls. It makes a grandmother's heart glad and happy to be included in the achievements of my grandchildren as they celebrate their academic pursuits. But there is nothing more gratifying to a grandparent than to see our grown children's children be grounded on the solid rock of Christ Jesus. It does indeed bring peace to our hearts knowing that our teachings of the gospel of Christ to our children are being passed to our grandchildren. How blessed we are.

PRAYER FOCUS:
The foundation your children or grandchildren are being raised upon

PRAYER:
Dear Father, we pray for our children, our grandchildren, all the children and young people today. We pray that they may have Godly upbringing and abiding peace within their homes. In Jesus' name. Amen.

THOUGHT FOR TODAY:
How can I express my love for my child/grandchild today?

GOD'S PLANS ARE GREATER THAN OURS

READ: Luke 12

*"Fear not, little flock, for it is your Father's good
pleasure to give you the kingdom"*
Luke 12:32 RSV

There are times in our lives when it seems as though God is giving us more than we can stand. We begin to question His intentions, and ask why. But we must remember to see God's actions in our lives from a different perspective. One of hope. When our lives are seemingly being tossed about, God is making great changes for us. We must remember to move forward with whatever challenge we are facing, because we can be assured that God cares, and is attending to every detail of our lives, today, tomorrow and eternally.

PRAYER FOCUS:
May God reveal his plans

PRAYER:
*Dear Father, thank you for the times of discomfort. May we remember
that in time you will transform us, and we must trust your plan
because we are your flock, and we shall not fear. In your name, Amen.*

THOUGHT FOR TODAY:
How is God working through a current episode for his greater purpose?

GOD IS IN CONTROL

READ Psalm 93

The Lord reigns; he is robed in majesty;
the Lord is robed, he is girded with strength.
Yea, the world is established; it shall never be moved;
thy throne is established from of old;
thou art from everlasting.
The floods have lifted up, O Lord,
the floods have lifted up their voice,
the floods lift up their roaring.
Mightier than the thunders of many waters,
mightier than the waves of the sea,
the Lord on high is mighty!
Thy decrees are very sure;
holiness befits thy house,
O Lord, for evermore. Psalm 93:1-5 RSV

If God is in control, then why do things go wrong? God is in control, but things go wrong because God doesn't force his subjects to worship, and there are those who chose not to. This is to encourage you that no matter what your life is like right now, and despite all the difficulties and the times when things go wrong, be affirmed that God is on the throne and He is in control. You can believe and trust that he will see you through. The psalms are full of praises to our god, comfort for your heart and peace for your life. Find your favorite ones—read them and meditate on them, and prayerfully offer up to God your prayers and concerns. He cares for you.

PRAYER FOCUS:
God is in control

PRAYER:
Dear Father, we affirm that you are majestic and mighty and created this world and are still in control. Let us praise and worship you and seek you in the quietness of our hearts. In Jesus' name. Amen.

THOUGHT FOR TODAY:
Find peace in God's ways

THE CROSS

READ: John 3:16

*For God so loved the world that he gave his only Son,
so that everyone who believes in him may not perish
but may have eternal life.* John 3:16 NRSV

We sometimes confuse the way the cross is perceived. It is the symbol of Christianity, and is often depicted in common places. Earrings, necklaces, rings, wall decorations, doodles in the margin of a notebook. We see the cross so often that we become desensitized to it. What happened on the cross changed the world forever. And it is important to remember and appreciate what our jewelry symbolizes. If God so loved the world and gave his one and only son to die for our sins so that we may live, then this symbol goes much deeper than jewelry. When the cross is portrayed in the media or in movies, we should not shy away from the imagery. We should turn our attention toward it and contemplate that Christ was fulfilling His reason for coming to earth. As difficult as it may be, the message of hope is that the story does not end there. We do not have to shy away from the cross because Jesus does not stay dead, the tomb is empty. The resurrection means there is victory over death. We, as Christians, are fortunate to be a part of this ever-unfolding true story of the life, death and resurrection of Christ.

PRAYER FOCUS:
Jesus' sacrifice on the cross

PRAYER:

Dear Father, thank you for the Cross of Jesus Christ. Let us be prayerful. Let us be your witness in the world today, sharing our faith with those who are in the dark. In Jesus' name. Amen.

THOUGHT FOR TODAY:

How can I embrace the death and resurrection of Jesus today?

DISAPPOINTMENT

READ: Job 3

Why is life given to a man
Whose way is hidden,
Whom God has hedged in?
For sighing has become my daily food;
My groans pour out like water.
Job 3:23-24 NIV

For those of you who are suffering undue disappointment in your life, these points of view will hopefully give you a new perspective. If people disappoint you, if your own mistakes disappoint you, if your faith appears a little weak during disappointment, if you feel life is unfair, and if you think that disappointment is your way of life, believe in Easter Sunday once again for hope and light. Your focus will begin to turn to the knowledge that through Christ, we have the strength to move past our disappointments. He gives us strength to overcome the disappointments of life. We remember the life of Jesus, the disappointments he witnessed as everyone rejected him as he was put to death, but we take heart that he became the ultimate example to us by overcoming death itself.

PRAYER FOCUS:
We have hope in Christ

PRAYER:

Dear Father, thank you for the hope in Christ that lets us overcome disappointment in whatever form it comes into our lives. In Jesus' name. Amen.

THOUGHT FOR TODAY:

In our darkest disappointments, Jesus is there with us

DISCIPLINE WITH LOVE

READ: Hebrews 12

And you have forgotten the exhortation that addresses you as children—
"My child, do not regard lightly the discipline of the Lord,
or lose heart when you are punished by him;
For the Lord disciplines those whom he loves,
And chastises every child whom he accepts."
Hebrews 12:5-7 NRSV

So often we hear stories on the news of unspeakable violence from children, teens, or young adults who seem to be out of control with their behavior. Parents and teachers seem at a loss of what the next step of discipline should be. What are you left with when you feel you've tried everything and the behavior only escalates? We tend to find ourselves assigning blame: the changing times, the media, turmoil within the family unit, peer pressures. . . If our youth are in crisis today, then we as parents, teachers and figures of authority need to know how to discipline with love. And we must discipline our youth because we love them. Prayer is the greatest tool. We must call upon the Lord to intervene in the lives of our children and protect them, and guide us to discipline with love.

PRAYER FOCUS:
How does God want me to react to my child?

PRAYER:
Dear Father, we fall on our knees for the youth of America.
We ask for the wisdom to know how to guide these precious

souls in the ways of righteousness. And let our youth know that
we truly love them even as you love them so much more.
In Jesus' name. Amen.

THOUGHT FOR TODAY:

Despite age and generation, we can still connect and relate with our
children. Find ways to intentionally spend time with your children today

THE SEED IS THE WORD OF GOD

READ: Luke 8

Now the parable is this: The seed is the word of God. The ones along the path are those who have heard; then the devil comes and takes away the word from their hearts, that they may not believe and be saved. And the ones on the rock are those who, when they hear the word, receive it with joy; but these have no root, they believe for a while and in time of temptation fall away. And as for what fell among the thorns, they are those who hear, but as they go on their way they are choked by the cares and riches and pleasures of life, and their fruit does not mature. And as for that in the good soil, they are those who, hearing the word, hold it fast in an honest and good heart, and bring forth fruit with patience. Luke 8:11-15 RSV

The first time I planted heirloom tomato seeds, I took care and placed them in peat pots under grow lights and covered them with a clear top for a greenhouse effect. When they sprouted three days later I showed them to my husband triumphantly and he replied, "They have a good environment in which to grow." In the controlled environment I created for the tomato seeds, I left them no choice but to sprout and grow. We must do the same for the seeds that God plants in our hearts. In our lives, we have choices to make as God plants his seeds in our hearts through his word. We can choose to let them be snatched away by the world's temptations. We can let our enthusiasm of the Word get crowded out by worries of tomorrow, making money and having a good time, or we can choose to plant the seed of the Word of God in the good earth of our hearts and let God bring that seed to abundant harvest!

PRAYER FOCUS:

Give me patience to let the seeds God has planted grow

PRAYER:

Dear Father, let our hearts be ready to choose to plant your words in the good earth for an abundant harvest. In Jesus' name. Amen

THOUGHT FOR TODAY:

Where is God working and planting seeds in your life?

QUIET SPACE

READ: Proverbs 1

But whoever listens to me will live in safety
And be at ease, without fear of harm.
Proverbs 1:33 NIV

It is important that we find our quiet place, and listen to God through scripture reading, meditate upon his word, and pray through life's challenges because in our quiet space we gain security. The fear of the unknown in the world will lose its grip. If you are struggling with finding that quiet space each day, pray that God will reveal it to you, and show you just where, when, and how. God is faithful and desires this time with you each day. He is waiting for you...

PRAYER FOCUS:
Quiet my heart to hear God speak

PRAYER:
Dear Father, Thank you for your faithfulness to us each
day. Thank you for each time we set aside for a 'talk'
with you and let us truly desire that closeness.
In Jesus' name. Amen.

THOUGHT FOR TODAY:
When can I take a few minutes to be at peace
and know that God is with me?

THE HIGHWAY OF LIFE

———

READ: **Psalm 46:10**

"Be still, and know that I am God.
I am exalted among the nations,
I am exalted in the earth!"
Psalm 46:10 NRSV

When I reflect upon the deep meaning of these words, I am convinced that God does want us to stop what we are doing and be still and know that God is God. We can do nothing lasting or of value on this earth without His guiding hand. So, I am reminded to step out of traffic and take a long look at God. This can speak volumes to many of us, as we are in the fast lane of traffic literally each day of the week. We are confronted on each side with the road rage of other drivers that frustrates us and makes us anxious on the highway of life. We cannot control their behavior, but we can make wise choices regarding ours. We can pray for others to be still and know that God is God.

PRAYER FOCUS:
Give me the strength to be still

PRAYER:
Dear Father, today, as we face the new day, help us, guide us, to be still and know that you are god in the most real sense. Let us know your peace that comes from taking time out of our busy lives to acknowledge you as our refuge, to be exalted among all nations. In Jesus' name. Amen.

THOUGHT FOR TODAY:
Slow down and find God in places you never expected

THE POWER OF A WORD

READ James 3:1-12

But no human being can tame the tongue—
a restless evil, full of deadly poison.
With it we bless the Lord and Father, and with it we curse men,
Who are made in the likeness of God. James 3:8-9 RSV

Do we really understand how powerful our words are? In times of stress, when things are not going well, how tempting is it to say something that doesn't reflect Christ's love? If we were to keep a written record of our words today, would more of them be hurtful or helpful? My husband has a custom at Christmastime, a busy time for many, of handing out small candy canes. These can bring a smile to the face of a frustrated store clerk, reassurance to a lonely stranger, or utter glee to a small child. And with these candy canes, goes a message, the word that "God loves you." Let us resolve daily and especially in times of stress, to use words of praise and encouragement, forgiveness and love.

PRAYER FOCUS:
Help me to be slow to speak and thoughtful to respond

PRAYER:
Dear Father, We thank you for this gentle reminder that our words are indeed powerful and lasting. Let us build each other up in the body of Christ as we focus on those words being helpful, kind and loving.
In Jesus' name. Amen.

THOUGHT FOR TODAY:
Who will I affect with my words today? Will it be to uplift or tear them down?

THE JOY OF SORROW

READ: Ecclesiastes 7

Sorrow is better than laughter,
For by sadness of countenance the heart is made glad.
Ecclesiastes 7:3 NRSV

I often start my day with Ecclesiastes 3. It is good to reflect on God's timing and to know there is "time for everything". Ecclesiastes is filled with Godly wisdom, a philosophy of life, and how God fits into it. Ecclesiastes shows us how to find spiritual significance in a life that would otherwise be meaningless. Ecclesiastes is a deep and thought-provoking part of the Bible. It asks the hard questions, shows the unembellished life of a sinful world. It offers a glimpse at the secular mind. It looks at suffering and struggles, and finds meaning in it all. But most importantly, in the end, Ecclesiastes points us to an eternal solution in Christ.

PRAYER FOCUS:
May God grant me a desire to study scripture
and know His word deeper and deeper

PRAYER:
Dear Father, thank you for the book of Ecclesiastes. Thank
you for the writer who shows a reverence toward life. Help
us with our doubts, struggles and fear of everyday life to find
solace in the reading of this book of wisdom and guidance.
In Jesus' name. Amen.

THOUGHT FOR TODAY:
How can I turn a sad situation into one that manifests the joy of the Lord

THE BLESSINGS THAT COUNT

READ **Proverbs 10**

The blessing of the Lord brings wealth,
Without painful toil for it. Proverbs 10:22 NIV

When a string of gloomy late-fall days, that are rainy and cold, are punctuated by a bright, warm, lovely day, that is full of sunshine, my spirit cannot help but be lifted. Such was the case yesterday. And I thought that this wonderful weather change would have brought a cheerful attitude in the people I met yesterday. Somehow, it did not! I felt discouraged that more people failed to see God's beautiful day as a blessing. So when the good days come and God's blessings are revealed we must encourage those around us to see the joy of the Lord's work. As we examine our own mental state, it's good to know that the blessing of the Lord makes us rich, not in material possessions but in life's intangibles, our true blessings of sunny days, family, home, faith and health.

PRAYER FOCUS:
Grant me eyes to see God's blessings around me

PRAYER:
Dear Father, thank you for giving the scriptures that reveal the meaning of real blessings in our lives. Help us to think on these things and give praise for the riches you bring to us each in our blessings. Let our emotions be changed from depressed to joyful when your blessings are revealed. In Jesus' name. Amen.

THOUGHT FOR TODAY:
What new blessings is God bringing into your life?
How can you make sure you don't miss them?

JESUS CALMS OUR STORMS

READ **Luke 8**

One day he got into a boat with his disciples, and he said to them,
"Let us go across to the other side of the lake." So they set out,
and as they sailed he fell asleep. And a storm of wind came down
on the lake, and they were filling with water, and were in danger.
And they went and woke him, saying, "Master, Master, we are
perishing!" And he awoke and rebuked the wind and the raging
waves; and they ceased, and there was a calm. He said to them,
"Where is your faith?" And they were afraid, and they marveled,
saying to one another, "Who then is this, that he commands even
wind and water, and they obey him?" Luke 8:22-25 RSV

It is important to call this story to mind in times of turmoil and uncertainty. There was time when wildfires became a very real threat to my son who lives in California. Our family prayed for the winds to change and spare my son's home. Our prayers were answered and the wind did change. But then our thoughts turned toward the many other homes and businesses that were destroyed in the wake of the fire, and we prayed that God would continue to intervene with miracles of rain to end this nightmare for so many people. We know that God still works miracles in our world today, just as He did with His disciples in calming the storm in their boat when they felt like they were perishing. And we must remember to trust that He has control, and He will calm the storms of our lives.

PRAYER FOCUS:
In what way have you taken too much control of your
life? What do you need to hand over to God?

PRAYER:

Dear Father, we pray in the name of Jesus Christ that you will bring relief to those who are suffering. That you would bring a miracle. Please be with us as we fight our battles, and please let those who do not know you, turn to you and be saved.

THOUGHT FOR TODAY:

Give God control of the storm in front of you

FROM SEEDLING TO BLOOM

READ: Matthew 6

Therefore I tell you, do not worry about your life, what
you will eat or drink; or about your body, what you will
wear. Is not life more than food, and the body more than
clothing? Look at the birds of the air; they do not sow nor
reap nor gather into barns, and yet your heavenly Father feeds
them. Are you not of more value than they? And can any
of you by worrying add a single hour to you span of life?
Matthew 6:25-27 NRSV

I once nurtured a plant that was given to me as a tiny seedling. I
did not know its name, and I curiously observed as it grew in the
shaded area of my garden to become a lovely green one-stalk plant.
Later, I moved it into the greenhouse for winter and there it began
to bud. It progressed daily until about a week later, the gorgeous
bloom gradually opened. It revealed a dark purple bulb but as it
began to unfold a magnificent white inner layer became visible. I
was excited to see how it gradually formed, according to God's plan
for its purpose. In its final burst of the complete bloom it was one
of the most beautiful single blooms I had ever seen. Dark purple
outside and pure white within, in a perfectly rounded trumpet
shape. Its perfume seemed as if the fragrance of Christ had entered
the greenhouse. I was awed and amazed. I later discovered that it
was called a Daytura Plant, or trumpet plant, aptly named for its
shape. It was a beauty to behold.

As I watched the progression and ultimate maturation of this
plant from seedling to bloom, I was able to appreciate God's timing,
and patiently observe as his plans for it unfolded. There are times

in our lives when it seems as though the bloom comes quickly. But often we spend too much time worrying about the end product and forget to enjoy the beauty of the growth. Remember that God works beauty is shown throughout the entirety of the process if we have eyes to see it.

PRAYER FOCUS:
Give us eyes to see and hearts full of patience

PRAYER:
Dear Father, how great and awesome your presence with us each day in the way you unfold nature's glory to our senses. Thank you for allowing us to see you in such unexpected ways as a flower's bloom. Your creation fills us with awe as we learn to see you in every moment of it. We thank you for this incredible gift of life in your creation. In Jesus name. Amen.

THOUGHT FOR TODAY:
In a moment of anxiety, step back and take in God's creation all around you

SHINE LIKE A STAR

READ: **Philippians 2**

Do everything without grumbling or arguing, so that you may become blameless and pure, "children of God without fault in warped and crooked generation." Then you will shine among them like stars in the sky as you hold firmly to the word of life. And then I will be able to boast on the day of Christ that I did not run or labor in vain.
Philippians 2:14-16 NIV

All my life I have been told to shine like a star for Christ. As an adult, it has become even more imperative to shine like a star in a darkened world that is scary at times. It is a daily challenge to remember our calling and purpose—to be a light for others, to gain encouragement from how we live as Christians.

I remember I once engaged in an activity where stickers of stars were awarded for certain behaviors, and in the end, whoever had the most stars won a prize. I marveled at the work others put in to achieve this prize. How often do we take seriously the challenges and opportunities God offers us each day? Jesus calls us to be a light to nations. We have been given an incredible example in the life of Jesus. We should not try to outshine other stars, but focus on the light we can offer to those in darkness.

PRAYER FOCUS:
What type of light am I offering?

PRAYER:
Dear Father, thank you for the gift of being a shining star in the darkened world. Help us to seek to light the path

for those who are stumbling in the dark in everything that we do, every day. In Jesus' name, Amen.

THOUGHT FOR TODAY:
How can I bring light into the lives of those around me as I go about my day?

EMBRACE THE SPECIAL MOMENTS

READ: **Psalm 103**

But the steadfast love of the Lord is from everlasting to everlasting
on those who fear him, and his righteousness to children's children,
To those who keep his covenant and remember to do his commandments.
Psalm 103:17-18 NRSV

Righteousness influences generations to come in positive ways. When my grandsons were 10 and 12, they came to visit my husband and me. They were such well-mannered young boys with good Christian values. As I reflected on that time spent with them and the activities we shared, I at last thought of taking them to Sunday school, and church. They took a keen interest in the sermon, which was a blessing to behold. Several days later the 12 year old asked me about Heaven, and my thoughts about what it would be like. I marveled to share with him that I think it will be a supremely happy place where we will be Jesus and all our family and friends and we will live in our heavenly homes. It will be a continuation of our life on earth in a glorious and heavenly fashion. His eyes shone and it was such a special and sacred time that God allowed me to share with him my deep faith in the world to come.

PRAYER FOCUS:
Thank God for the gift of eternal life

PRAYER:
Dear Father, thank you for the honor and privilege of being parents
and grandparents. Help us always to take these roles seriously,

always knowing that what we are passing down to them will
one day be passed on to their children and grandchildren.
What an awesome responsibility!
In Jesus' name. Amen.

THOUGHT FOR TODAY:
*How does the knowledge of our eternal resting
place affect our lives today?*

A MEDITATION ON COMPASSION

READ Matthew 9

And Jesus went about all the cities and villages, teach in
their synagogues and preaching the gospel of the kingdom,
and healing every disease and every infirmity.
When he saw the crowds, he had compassion for them, because
they were harassed and helpless, like sheep without a shepherd.
Then he said to his disciples, "The harvest is plentiful, but
the laborers are few; pray therefore the Lord of the harvest to
send out laborers into his harvest." Mathew 9:35-38 RSV

Have you had to opportunity to show compassion in your week? If so, how did you respond? Were you like Jesus and felt moved to help someone who was harassed and helpless? How often are we presented with opportunities to show compassion to others in our lives? But do we always respond as Jesus would to someone who is harassed and helpless?

I am reminded of a time when I witnessed a young mother at the mercy of her misbehaving young child as she was attempting to register for classes at a local college. She was unable to concentrate, and the child was crying, whining and touching things he shouldn't. Though she threatened him with punishment, his torment persisted, and culminated with his overturning a cup and spilling soda all over the floor. I hesitated to intervene, my actions stopped by pressures to not get involved with parent-child misbehavior problems. Finally, an employee came to the rescue, helped clean the mess and distract the child so his mother could finish registering for classes. In retrospect, I had an opportunity to show compassion, and to offer her my assistance, or a few brief words of encouragement. I let the moment pass me by. What would you have done? The good news is that God gives us all second chances to help someone in a helpless situation, and I will call to mind this experience in the future. My prayer is that God will use this example from my life, and encourage someone else when the situation arises for them to show compassion.

PRAYER FOCUS:
How can I show compassion to those around me?

PRAYER:
Dear Father, thank you for the opportunities to show compassion to the helpless and harassed. Let our hearts, souls, minds and spirits respond to those who need help, sympathy, pity and most of all compassion.
In Jesus' name. Amen.

THOUGHT FOR TODAY:
Who needs compassion in my life?

A NEW DAY

READ **Psalm 5**

In the morning Lord, you hear my voice;
In the morning I lay my requests before you and wait expectantly.
Psalm 5:3 NIV

For some, morning is the best part of the day. To wake up with birds before sunrise when the world is quiet, fresh, and full of unusual sounds. There is a different feel, smell and taste. Even in the heat of summertime mornings can be a sacred time to be alone with God in his cool and welcoming presence. This is a time to find solitude and peace with our creator. A time to listen as He gives insight into his word. It is a time for prayer, meditation, and reflection upon all that God has planned. Mornings are a beautiful gift from God. Indeed, I am thankful for the dawning of a new day.

PRAYER FOCUS:
Give me focus on you, Lord, as I start my day

PRAYER:
Dear Father, let this new day bring forth all the beauty and joy
that you have planned for our lives. Let us find those special times
alone with you to discover the beauty of your glorious mornings.
In Jesus' name. Amen.

THOUGHT FOR TODAY:
What insight will I share from my time with God this morning?

A DEVOTION FOR COMFORT

READ: **Psalm 91**

He who dwells in the shelter of the Most High,
who abides in the shadow of the Almighty,
will say to the Lord, "My refuge and my fortress;
my God, in whom I trust."
For he will deliver you from the snare of the fowler
and from the deadly pestilence;
He will cover you with his pinions,
and under his wings you will find refuge;
his faithfulness is a shield and buckler.
You will not fear the terror of the night,
nor the arrow that flies by day
Psalm 91:1-5 RSV

Animals are known for the fierce protection they give their young. We can be assured that God feels the same protectiveness for us. God's protection is like a shield to gather beneath in times of uncertainty. We must remember to praise God for the wonderful protection he gives in the metaphor of being shielded beneath the wings of a bird, and for the solidness of his shield that protects us from the world. For all who are suffering, with issues of health, relationships or strife, let us be comforted for a moment by these verses in Psalms. And humbly bow to His protection.

PRAYER FOCUS:
Those in need of comfort and healing

Dear Father, thank you for this passage of comfort. We praise you for the wonderful protection that you give. Help us to remember as go through trying times that you are shielding us. In Jesus' name. Amen.

THOUGHT FOR TODAY:

Who needs to hear words of comfort today?

GOD'S WORD IN OUR HEARTS

READ: Psalm 119

I have hidden your word in my heart that I might not sin against you.
Psalm 119:11 NIV

When we memorize God's word, it shapes how we live our lives. As a little girl I loved going to Vacation Bible School every summer in our west Texas school-house church. And now when I see signs for Vacation Bible School all around the neighborhood where I live, I'm transported to those long, fun afternoons of VBS as a young girl. One of my favorite activities was taking a bible verse each day to memorize that night and recite the next day. Psalm 119:11 is one that has remained with me throughout my life. I think of that verse and thank God that it is firmly implanted in my mind and in my heart, so that my life might reflect it. I encourage people of all ages to keep up the practice of memorizing scriptures, so that His word echoes in our hearts and in our minds as we live our daily lives.

PRAYER FOCUS:
Thank God for the gift of his Word that we are able to memorize

PRAYER:
Dear Father, Today let us remember the words that you have hidden in our hearts as children. The verses that come to mind in times of trouble, joy and challenge. Let us share these treasured verses with the people that cross our paths and need encouragement. Let us remember most of all these words in our hearts, so that we might not sin against you. In Jesus' name. Amen.

What verse has been a beacon of hope for you? Decide and put it to memory

THE SWEETEST SCENT

READ: 2 Corinthians 2

But thanks be to God, who in Christ always leads us in triumphal procession, and through us spreads the in every place the fragrance that comes from knowing him. For we are the aroma of Christ to God among those who are being saved and among those who are perishing, to the one a fragrance from death to death, to the other a fragrance from like to life. Who is sufficient for these things?
2 Corinthians 2:14-16 NRSV

Recently, I met a woman who spoke of knowing only two people whose homes exuded the fragrance of Christ. She had known the moment she stepped inside their doors that the Fragrance of Christ was present. And I thought about those words. I delved deeper into the subject of the fragrance of Christ and its scriptural significance and found something profound and worth remembering in the above scriptures. As we go forward in our lives, let the fragrance of Christ precede us and envelop those we interact with in our witnessing for Christ Jesus' victory over death. It is our choice. Think of the sweetest fragrance you have ever known, and multiply that by a million and it will not be sweeter than the fragrance of Christ, because his fragrance is love, unconditional love, mercy, acceptance and forgiveness. It is yours if you will only ask.

PRAYER FOCUS:
Thank God for the fragrance of Christ

PRAYER:

Dear Father, let us go about with the fragrance of Christ in our life; in our personality, our spirit, our homes, as we are witnesses of Christ's victory over sin and the promise of abundant life in him. In Jesus' name. Amen.

THOUGHT FOR TODAY:

How do I practically exhibit Christ's fragrance to those around me?

FACING FEAR

READ: Mathew 8

And when he got into the boat, his disciples followed him. And behold, there arose a great storm on the sea, so that the boat was being swamped by the waves; but he was asleep. And they went and woke him, saying, "Save us, Lord; we are perishing." And he said to them, "Why are you afraid, O men of little faith?" Then he rose and rebuked the winds and the seas; and there was a great calm. And the men marveled, saying, "What sort of man is this, that even the winds and seas obey him?"
Mathew 8:23-27 RSV

Does having faith mean that we will never be afraid? Once in a Bible study, one woman asked me "Is there a general feeling of being overwhelmed with the fears of life?" I replied, "Definitely!" But then explained that we must not despair because, as scripture tells us, our faith can move mountains as long as we have it. Whatever fear you are facing today, just remember that we have a God that is much bigger than that fear. If you doubt that, just go outside tonight and look up at the stars in place in the universe! He put them there just like He put you here on this earth. He loves and cares so deeply for you. You matter to God. Keep your faith strong in Christ Jesus.

PRAYER FOCUS:
Let God's love overwhelm you as you pray

PRAYER:

Dear Father, whatever fears we are facing today, let us remember your promise that you are there, we are not alone. Let us trust You more. In Jesus' name. Amen.

THOUGHT FOR TODAY:

Doubt and fear do not defeat us if we place our faith and hope in Christ

RELATIONSHIPS

READ: Ephesians 5:22-24

Wives, submit yourselves to you own husbands as you do to the Lord.
For the husband is the head of the wife as Christ is the head of the church,
His body, of which he is the Savior.
Ephesians 5:22-23 NIV

When the media is focused on war, and images and stories of troops dominate the programming, I am drawn to the stories about spouses, separating to serve overseas. We must keep in our hearts and minds our troops and pray for their protection as they protect us, we must also keep our loved ones on the home front in focus. I encourage you as husbands and wives to take to heart what the scriptures tell us about husband-wife relationships. As we see the tearful departures of spouses and loved ones to serve overseas, we realize even more the importance of honoring each other in our day-to-day interactions. Husbands, love your wives, just as Christ loved the church and gave himself for her. Wives, submit to your own husband, as to the Lord.

PRAYER FOCUS:
Pray for your spouse or a loved one

PRAYER:
Dear Father, Let us take to heart the precious time we are given each day
with our spouses and loved ones. Let them be honored as you are honored.
In Jesus' name. Amen.

THOUGHT FOR TODAY:
How can I express my love for my spouse today through service?

OUR GREATEST WEAPON

READ: Joshua 1

*Only be strong and very courageous, being careful to do
according to all the law which Moses my servant commanded
you; turn not from it to the right hand or to the left, that you
may have good success wherever you go.* Joshua 1:7 RSV

During the early years of America's involvement in the Middle East,
I was working as a chaplain and given a list of names of soldiers
in combat to lift up in prayer. Having real names and real faces
connected me to real families that brought my prayers into sharp
focus. God has given each of us a certain responsibility during this
time of war. Each day we know that prayers are indeed, our greatest
weapon of war. I encourage you to seek God in all His wisdom for
your life as our lives are changing all the time. I encourage you to
pray for wisdom in your decisions and choices this day. I encourage
you to pray for the leaders of our country and the world for Godly
wisdom in their decisions. Prayer is our most effective and powerful
weapon against the forces of evil that lurk in our war-torn world.

PRAYER FOCUS:
Pray for those who have felt the consequences of war most intensely

PRAYER:
*Dear Father, we pray for wisdom for our soldiers. We pray for our
leaders, and their advisors, all our troops, for divine wisdom and the
peace that passes understanding in whatever outcome of these days.
In Jesus' name. Amen.*

THOUGHT FOR TODAY:

Is there a family you know that continues to sacrifice for the service of their country? How can you show gratefulness to them today?

GOOD WORK

READ: **Philippians 1:1-11**

I am confident of this, that the one who began a good
work among you will bring it to completion by the
day of Jesus Christ. Philippians 1:6 NRSV

What work will God finally complete in us? What a marvelous promise of truth that we can hold dear in our stress filled lives and world. Sometimes we may forget that God is working in our lives amid the stresses of worry, fears, financial burdens, friendships gone sour, and much more. However, we must continue to look on the bright side of our lives and not let the adversary steal our joy. We must readjust our focus and look to the Lord Jesus who can calm our hearts in times of stress that seem unbearable. It is vital to set aside a time each day...morning, noon, or night to reconnect with God. Prayer, studying the Scriptures, and meditation works every time!

PRAYER FOCUS:
God, show us where you are working in our lives

PRAYER:
Dear Father. Thank you for this day. Help us to know that
we can cope with whatever stresses that come. Help us
to know that true joy can be found if we seek You.
In Jesus' name. Amen.

THOUGHT FOR TODAY:
How can I show the joy of God today?

MAKE SCRIPTURE YOUR PRAYER

READ **Philippians 4**

Finally, brethren, whatever is true, whatever is honorable, whatever is just, whatever is pure, whatever is lovely, whatever is gracious, if there is any excellence, if there is anything worthy of praise, think about these things. Philippians 4:8 RSV

How can we think lovely thoughts? So often discouraging thoughts can control our thinking. We must choose to discipline our thoughts. How is your thinking today? If you are struggling with feelings or thoughts of discouragement or depression/sadness, perhaps it's time to get into the Word of God. Pray for the Holy Spirit to lead you to the scriptures that you most need to read. Looking in the Index to Subjects in a study bible may be a way to start your journey. As you find verses that speak to you, write them down or try to put them to memory. Reading and claiming scripture can become a prayer.

PRAYER FOCUS:
God, give us a desire to study scripture

PRAYER:
Dear Father, Thank you for your Holy Word, the Holy Scriptures that You have given for our every need. Thank you that we can turn our thoughts of discouragement to thoughts of encouragement in whatever we are going through. Bless us as we explore Your Word today. In Jesus' name. Amen.

THOUGHT FOR TODAY:
The more often we open scripture the quicker it will come to mind in our moments of need

THE LOVE CHAPTER

READ: 1 Corinthians 13

Love is patient, love is kind. It does not envy, it does not boast,
it is not proud. It does not dishonor others, it is not self-seeking,
it is not easily angered, it keeps no record of wrongs. Love
does not delight in evil but rejoices with the truth. It always
protects, always trusts, always hopes, always perseveres.
I Corinthians 13:4-7 NIV

With Valentine's week upon us, our hearts are turned to expressing our love for sweethearts, spouses, parents, children, grandchildren, friends, family or perhaps even a stranger. It is good to reflect on 1 Corinthians 13. We gain new insight into what real love is according to Paul. It will bring us back to why we are to love with patience, kindness, free of envy, never boastful or proud, never rude, never self-seeking, and is not easily angered. Love rejoices in truth. It always protects, always trusts, always hopes, and always endures. These words from the Lord are truly words to live by today, this week and for a life time.

PRAYER FOCUS:
God, grant us a desire to love as you have called us to love

PRAYER:
Dear Father, Today we come to Your presence with a heart full
of love that transcends all human emotions. Let us remember
those who may have been forgotten this week, those that
need extra love in their lives. In Jesus' name. Amen.

THOUGHT FOR TODAY:
How have I done recently at showing others love?

VOLUNTEERING FROM THE HEART

READ: James 2:14-24

*What good is it, my brothers and sisters, if you say you have
faith but do not have works? Can faith save you? If a brother or
sister is naked and lacks daily food, and one of you says to them,
"Go in peace; keep warm and eat your fill," and yet you do not
supply their bodily needs, what is the good of that? So faith by
itself, if it has no works, is dead.* James 2:14-17 NRSV

During the holidays, many chose to give their time and volunteer
at the Salvation Army posts, soup kitchens, nursing homes, or
homeless shelters. The question comes to mind: are we doing this
because of our faith in the Lord Jesus and from our hearts? Are
doing it out of duty or is this a true measure of our faith? I believe
as true Christians and disciples, we should do these things not only
at Christmas, but all year long! I encourage you, if you have not
volunteered in something that will give back to the poor, needy,
lonely, forgotten of society, to do so now. Nursing homes welcome
volunteers and need your help. You will certainly be a blessing as
you forget about your agenda for a time, and do good work for
others.

PRAYER FOCUS:
Grant me a heart of service

PRAYER:
*Dear Father, Thank you for the opportunities of volunteer service
in Your kingdom, especially as we see the overwhelming needs
of people all around us. Let us go forth in our faith, and do*

the lasting deeds that will make a difference in the lives of the
poor, the lonely, and the forgotten. In Jesus' name. Amen.

THOUGHT FOR TODAY:

What can I sacrifice this week to give back to my community?

HE WHO FIRST LOVED US

READ: 1 John 2

He who says he abides in him ought to walk in the same way in
which he walked. Beloved, I am writing you no new commandment,
but an old commandment which you had from the beginning;
the old commandment is the word which you have heard.
1 John 2:6-7 RSV

It is easy to love some people because they are easy to love. How do
we love those who are unlovable? It is not easy to love someone if
we disagree with their behavior, or their choices. But it is a critical
choice we must make, to love others as Jesus loves us. It takes
effort, and intention. As you go into your daily activities and face
many different types of people who make many different types of
choices—try and remember this verse of scripture, and walk in the
way in which He walked.

PRAYER FOCUS:
Grant us a heart of love greater than our own

PRAYER:
Dear Father, Today as we go out into our workplaces,
marketplaces, home places, let us remember to walk as Jesus
did and follow His example of truly loving our brother and
sister, with a spirit of forgiveness and cheerfulness.
In Jesus' name. Amen.

THOUGHT FOR TODAY:
Who is the person you find it hardest to love? How would God respond to them?

GIFTS OF THE SPIRIT

READ: 1 Corinthians 12

*Now there are varieties of gifts, but the same Spirit; and there are
varieties of service, but the same Lord; and there are varieties of
working, but it is the same God who inspires them all in every one.
To each is given the manifestation of the Spirit for the common good.
To one is given through the Spirit the utterance of wisdom, and to
another the utterance of knowledge according to the same Spirit, to
another faith by the same Spirit, to another gifts of healing by the
one Spirit, to another the working of miracles, to another prophecy,
to another the ability to distinguish between spirits, to another
various kinds of tongues, to another the interpretation of tongues.
All these are inspired by one and the same Spirit, who apportions
to each one individually as he wills.* 1 Corinthians 12:4-11 RSV

Have you discovered your spiritual gift? Has God revealed to you
how you can best serve Him through gifts that He has bestowed
on you? We all have spiritual gifts. They are given to us as a child
of God and He wants us to use them wisely and to build His
kingdom. I encourage you to search the scriptures and ask the Lord
to reveal to you your spiritual gifts. It is a grand responsibility and
privilege. You may be pleasantly surprised and rewarded by what
you discover.

PRAYER FOCUS:
Open our hearts to what gifts we can offer

PRAYER:

Dear Lord, please show us in the reading of these scriptures, prayer and meditation, just what gifts that You have given us. Let us use them always for Your glory. In Jesus' name. Amen.

THOUGHT FOR TODAY:

What gifts has God given you? How do you currently use that gift? Is it being used in an honorable way?

Printed in the United States
By Bookmasters